GO FOR IT! ™

TENNIS

FOR BOYS AND GIRLS

START RIGHT AND PLAY WELL

by Bill Gutman
with Illustrations
by Ben Brown

MARSHALL CAVENDISH
CORPORATION

GREY CASTLE PRESS

Marshall Cavendish Edition, Freeport, New York.

Published by arrangement with Grey Castle Press, Lakeville, Ct.

Copyright © 1990 by Grey Castle Press.

The *GO FOR IT* Sports Series is a trademark of Grey Castle Press.

Printed in the USA

The Library of Congress Cataloging in Publication Data

Gutman, Bill.
    Tennis : start right and play well / by Bill Gutman ; with
illustrations by Ben Brown.
        p.   cm. — (Go for it!)
   Summary: Describes the history and current teams, leagues, and
championships of tennis and provides instruction on how to play the
game.
   ISBN 0-942545-88-5 (lib. bdg.)
   1. Tennis—Juvenile literature. [1. Tennis.] I. Brown, Ben,
1921–   Ill. II. Title. III. Series: Gutman, Bill. Go for it!
GV996.5.G87   1990
796.342'2—dc20   89-7607
                                                                       CIP
                                                                       AC

Photo credits: Duomo/Adam Stoltman, page 8, top; Focus On Sports, page 8, bottom, page 9; UPI/Bettmann, page 6.

Special thanks to: Bob Riemer, varsity tennis coach, Webutuck Junior/Senior High School, Amenia, N.Y.

Picture research: Omni Photo Communications, Inc.

ABOUT THE AUTHOR

Bill Gutman is the author of over 70 books for children and young adults. The majority of his titles have dealt with sports, in both fiction and non-fiction, including "how-to" books. His name is well-known to librarians who make it their business to be informed about books of special interest to boys and reluctant readers. He lives in Poughquag, New York.

ABOUT THE ILLUSTRATOR

Ben Brown's experience ranges from cartoonist to gallery painter. He is a graduate of the High School of Music & Art in New York City and the University of Iowa Art School. He has been a member of the National Academy of Design and the Art Students' League. He has illustrated government training manuals for the disadvantaged (using sports as themes), and his animation work for the American Bible Society won two blue ribbons from the American Film Festival. He lives in Great Barrington, Massachusetts.

In order to keep the instructions in this book as simple as possible, the author has chosen in most cases to use "he" to signify both boys and girls.

A BRIEF HISTORY

Like many other sports, tennis is a very old game. There is some evidence that the ancient Egyptians, Greeks and Persians played a game similar to tennis thousands of years ago. Then, around the 12th century, wealthy people in both France and England began to play an indoor game called court or royal tennis.

The word tennis come from the French word *tenetz*, or *tenez*. In 1873 a British officer, Major Walter Clopton Wingfield, introduced the game of lawn tennis, and the modern game of tennis was born.

Lawn tennis was first played on a court shaped like an hour glass. There was a high net on the court, which was outlined on a grass lawn. To play Major Wingfield's game well, a person had to have speed, be very agile and hit the ball with great accuracy. That's not so different from what it takes to play tennis today.

It wasn't long before the new game became popular with the younger people in England. Another British officer took some balls and rackets to the Island of Bermuda in 1874, and soon, people were playing there, too. That's when an American woman, Mary Ewing Outerbridge, saw the game for the first time. She bought some equipment and brought it back to her home on Staten Island in New York.

At first, her girl friends didn't feel it was ladylike to play the new game, but her brothers thought it was great. It didn't take long for the game to begin spreading in the United States. Soon there were courts in Nahant, Massachusetts; Newport, Rhode

Helen Wills Moody was the first great woman's star of American tennis. She played during the 1920s and 1930s, winning many championships. Notice the style of dress of the period.

Island; and Philadelphia, Pennsylvania. In 1879, the first tennis court appeared in Santa Monica, California.

Two years before, the English had held the first lawn tennis championship matches at the old Wimbleton Grounds near London. By that time the court had become rectangular in shape and the net had been lowered. The sport began to look very similar to the way it looks today.

From that point, tennis grew rapidly. The United States Lawn Tennis Association was founded in 1881, and that same year the first United States men's championships were held at Newport, Rhode Island. The first French championships were held in 1891, and the first Australian championships took place in 1905. The four championships listed above remain the major tournaments for men and women.

Even though women might have been a bit slower to take to the new sport than men, they weren't really far behind. The first United States women's championships were held in 1887 in Philadelphia, and women have been playing the sport with the same intensity as the men ever since.

From there, the game slowly spread the world over. However, most of the champions right up until the 1960s came from the four countries—England, France, the United States and Australia— that held the major championships. The sport really became well known in the 1920s, when the first group of great champions came on the scene.

Perhaps the most famous was Bill Tilden, the greatest player of his day. Tilden won the United States Championship six straight times from 1920–25 and again in 1929. He also won Wimbledon (the English championships) three times and became a living tennis legend.

There were also some great women players emerging at this time. Beginning in 1923, Helen Wills Moody won the U.S. title six

Ivan Lendl was the number one-ranked player in the world in the late 1980s. A native of Czechoslovakia, Lendl has become a United States citizen and lives in Greenwich, Connecticut.

Chris Evert won her first Wimbledon title in 1974, the same year as Jimmy Connors. She has been a consistent champion ever since. Chris uses the two-hand backhand and prefers to play a baseline game with long rallies.

Like Ivan Lendl, Martina Navratilova was a native of Czechoslovakia. She, too, became a great champion and had an intense rivalry with Chris Evert. Martina also became a U.S. citizen as she continued her great career.

times in seven years. She won seven U.S. titles in all, and won at Wimbledon eight times. But while Tilden and Moody might have helped put tennis on the map, there have been many more great stars down through the years, too many to mention here.

Until 1968, only amateur players could compete in the major tournaments. Players who became professionals to earn money by playing tennis could not enter Wimbledon or the U.S. championships. But this rule was hurting the growth of the game. Finally, in 1968, the tournaments were opened to both amateurs and professionals. Now all the great tennis players could compete against each other. The "open" format helped tennis to become the great sport that it is today.

Some of the great players in the 1980s have been Chris Evert, Martina Navratilova and Steffi Graf among the women, and Jimmy Connors, Bjorn Borg, John McEnroe and Ivan Lendl among the men. All have been great champions, carrying on in the tradition of those who came before.

ORGANIZED TENNIS

Tennis today is a sport that is played all year round, indoors and outdoors, on many different kinds of courts. The game was originally called lawn tennis because the court was always laid out on a neatly manicured lawn. But with so many people playing the game, grass courts became too difficult to maintain in many places. Today, the only major tournament played on grass is the All-England championships at Wimbledon. Other court surfaces include clay, cement and other kinds of man-made or synthetic surfaces.

The United States Tennis Association governs all organized competition in the United States. Tennis, of course, is more of an individual sport than a team sport, but there are many age-group tournaments throughout the country. Any youngster working with a coach and learning the game can probably find a USTA tournament in his or her area.

There is a National Schools Program sponsored by the USTA to teach tennis in physical education classes. The USTA also sponsors the National Junior Tennis League, which provides both instruction and competitions. The USTA is working hard to spread the game to everyone.

Besides being taught in schools, tennis is also taught at camps and in many parks around the country. There are even specialized tennis camps for youngsters who want to learn the sport from expert teachers in the field. Playing in an organized program is the best way to learn the game. A good coach will know the level of

10

play for each youngster and can match him with others of equal or slightly better ability.

Most secondary and high schools have tennis teams. While boys and girls can compete as individuals, they are also representing their teams. Doubles partners must also learn to play together as a team. Some players prefer doubles to singles tennis, and in this sense the sport is also a team game.

Perhaps the biggest prize in tennis as a team sport is the Davis Cup. Teams from many nations compete for the Cup once a year. There are four singles and one doubles match in a Davis cup round. The country winning any three of these matches advances in the tournament until only two countries remain. The winner of the final round gets the Davis Cup.

Like the major tournaments, the Davis Cup matches used to be for amateur players only. Today any player can represent his country in Davis Cup matches.

Organized tennis exists in nearly every country in the world, with the International Tennis Federation as the governing body. There is prize money offered at every tournament, and tennis pros fly all over the world to play.

The big four tournaments are still Wimbledon, the United States Open, the French Open and the Australian Open. Any player winning all four in the same year is said to have achieved the ''Grand Slam.'' American Don Budge was the first to do it in 1938, and the last was West Germany's Steffi Graf in 1988. In between, there have been a host of great players from many lands, all of whom have helped make tennis a major world sport.

The Game

Tennis is played on a rectangular court 78 feet long. A singles court is 27 feet wide; a doubles court is 36 feet wide. The extra four and a half feet on each side of the singles court are called the

11

alleys. The net across the center of the court should be exactly three feet high in the middle and three and a half feet at the posts, which are located several feet to the outside of each sideline.

There is a right and left service court on each side of the net. The service courts are divided by a line down the middle of the court that extends 21 feet from the net. Another line across the court at that point marks end of the service courts. The line across the back of the court is called the *baseline*. There is also a small center mark in the middle of the baseline. The server must stay on one side or the other of the center mark while serving.

Some tennis courts are considered ''faster'' than others. Grass courts, for instance, are very fast, meaning the ball moves faster when it hits the grass. Clay courts, like the ones used in the French Open, are considered slow. The ball doesn't have the same hop that it does on grass.

A tennis player has to adjust his game to the surface. Usually the hard-hitting players who like to charge the net are best on fast courts. They are sometimes called ''serve and volley'' players. Players who prefer to hit their shots from the baseline and try to win long rallies do better on a slow surface. They can reach most balls and wait until their opponents make a mistake.

New players should learn about the different kinds of surfaces so they can judge the skip and bounce of the tennis ball. This is especially true when playing on a new surface for the first time. The ball may not react the way it did on another surface.

The object of the game is relatively simple. The ball must always be hit on the fly or on one bounce within the confines of the court. It is put into play by serves, which must be made from behind the right or left side of the baseline into the service court on the opposite side. In other words, if a player is serving from the right side of the baseline, he must put the ball into the left service court. If he is serving from the left side, he must hit the ball into the right service court.

The player who is serving will alternate from the right to left side with each succeeding serve. He gets two chances to put the ball in play. If a serve goes into the net or is outside any of the lines of the service court, it is no good and called a *fault*. Two straight faults, called a *double fault*, result in the loss of a point. Then the server moves to the opposite side to try again.

Once a serve is in play and returned, the players contend for the point by hitting the ball back and forth over the net. To win a point, a player must either hit the ball past his opponent (making sure the ball bounces in the court) or force his opponent into making an error. An error can result from hitting the ball into the net or hitting it outside the boundary lines of the court.

To be called out, the ball must land completely outside the sideline or baseline. If it hits any part of the line, it remains in play. This goes for the serve as well. If the serve hits any part of a line on the serving court, it is good. A player should play any ball he is not sure about. If he stands around watching it, expecting it to be out, he may be in for a surprise.

Scoring in tennis is simple, but different. Many beginners may become confused because the terms are unusual and the numbering sequences unique to the sport. Like other net games, such as volleyball and ping pong, the scoring is in points. When a player gets enough points, he wins the game. When he wins enough games, he wins the set. When he wins enough sets, he wins the match.

Let's start from the beginning, with the terms. In tennis, zero, or nothing, is always referred to as *love*. Whenever the term is used, it means a player has not won a point, has not won a game or has not won a set.

It takes just four points to win a game in tennis. However, a player must always win by at least two points. So if the players are tied at three points each, the game will go until one player has at least five points. If they tie at five, it must go until at least seven. In fact, some long games can go to 20 or more points.

Points, however, are not counted, 1–2–3–4. The first point scored is referred to as 15. Remember, 15 means just one point. When calling out scores, the score of the server is always given first. So if the server wins the first point, the score is *15-love*, the equivalent of 1–0. If the server's opponent wins the first point, the score is given as *love-15*, also the equivalent of 1–0.

The second point is referred to as 30, and the third point won is called 40. So when a player scores points, he goes from 15 to 30, then to 40. That means he has scored three points.

Here are some quick examples. If the server has scored one point and his opponent two, the score is *15-30*. If the server has scored three points and his opponent none, the score is *40-love*. If both players have scored two points, the score is *30-30*, or *30-all*.

The next question is what happens when the score goes to *40-40*. After all, a player must win a game by at least two points. At *40-40*, the numerical scoring stops. Instead of *40-40*, the game is now at *deuce*, which means simply that the score is tied and one of the players must now win by two.

The game continues. The player winning the next point has the *advantage* or *ad*. If the server wins the point, he will call the score out as "my ad." If he loses the point he will say, "your ad," to his opponent. If there is an official announcing the score, he will say, "advantage, Mr. Jones," or "advantage, Mr. Smith," depending on who wins the point.

If the player with the advantage wins the next point, he has won the game. However, if his opponent wins the point, the game goes back to deuce. That means it is tied once again, and one of the players must still win by two points. At this point, there are no more numbers used. Even if the game were to go for fifty points, the only terms used are deuce for a tie and advantage for a one-point lead.

In most cases, a player must win six games to win a set. He can win by scores of 6–1, 6–4, or even 6–0 or 6-love. In the old days, players had to win sets by two games. So if a set was tied at 5–5, a player had to win two more games to win the sets. Sometimes sets could go for many, many games before someone won. It was not unusual to see sets of 15–13 or 21–19. Long sets such as those would lengthen a match and exhaust the players.

Now, when a set becomes tied at 6–6, a tiebreaker is used to decide the winner. In major tournaments, the first player to reach seven points wins the game and the set. In tiebreakers, the points are counted in numerical order, 1-2-3-4-5-6-7.

Just a word to wrap up the scoring. Most matches are decided by the best two-of-three sets. However, in many of the major tournaments, the men play a best three-of-five-set format. Many times a player who has lost the first two sets comes back to win the match. This takes a great deal of stamina, determination and mental toughness. But it's all part of the game.

As mentioned before, singles tennis is played on the smaller court, which is just 27 feet wide. It is strictly a one-on-one confrontation. In doubles, played on the 36 foot court, players must work together as a team. In major tournaments, there are men's and women's singles competitions, men's and women's doubles competitions and mixed doubles matches.

In mixed doubles, there is a man and woman on each team. This is normally the only time men and women play against each other on the tennis court. Some players prefer singles, others doubles. But many like to play both. It offers a change of pace and allows the player to really learn all phases of the game.

Getting Ready To Play

At first glance, a newcomer to the sport may not realize that to play tennis well, players of any age must be in tip-top physical condition. Tennis is a game of quickness. There is a great deal of stop and start action, a lot of bending and stretching, as well as all-out short sprints. It's the kind of sport in which an out-of-shape player can easily pull a muscle, strain his or her back or sustain a leg or ankle injury.

Because of the type of movement involved, tennis is not an easy game to play with an injury. Therefore, it's best for a young player to get into good physical condition and to stay that way. For starters, that means good day-to-day living habits, the right foods and plenty of rest. To play the game in a tired state is the same as playing out of condition. It makes it easy to get hurt.

The young player should also work to build up stamina. A long, three-set match is very tiring, especially in that third set. That means a young player should do aerobic exercises, such as running or jumping rope, on a regular basis. Jumping rope, for example, will help with coordination and footwork. And all tennis players need nimble feet to move around the court.

In addition, tennis players should constantly be doing stretching exercises for their arms, legs and back. Stretching should be part of their daily warm-up before practice sessions and before a match. The stretching exercises can be similar to those used by track and field athletes.

The tennis player may begin by placing his hands on his hips, legs spread apart and knees straight. He should then rotate his upper body at the hips in a circular motion. At the same time, he should stretch and bend to the front, then the side, next the back and finally the other side. The circular motion will loosen muscles in the back, sides and abdomen.

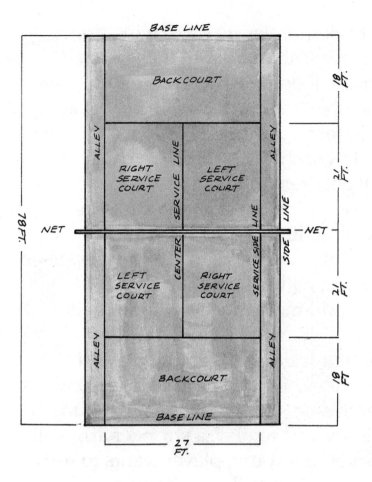

All tennis courts have the same dimensions. Only the surfaces may vary. The court is always 78 feet long. Singles courts are 27 feet wide. Doubles courts are 36 feet wide with the addition of two, 4½ foot alleys. The four-service courts are 21 feet deep and 13½ feet wide. The net is 3 feet high in the center and 3½ feet wide at the posts. Very few surfaces are still grass covered. Others are hard clay. But most surfaces today are either cement or a variety of synthetic materials.

Leg exercises can include basic toe touching. Feet wide apart and knees straight, the young athlete should touch the right hand to the left toe, then the left hand to the right toe, standing upright in between. The next warm-up can be a hamstring stretch, done by placing one leg out straight on some kind of support, like the back of a chair or a rail. With the other leg bent slightly at the knees, the athlete slowly slides both hands along the outstretched leg, bending at the waist. The closer the hands come to the foot, the more the hamstring stretches.

This exercise should be done several times with each leg. Like all stretching exercises, it should be done slowly, with the final, stretched position held for five to ten seconds. There should be a feeling of the muscle stretching, but little pain or discomfort.

A good exercise to loosen back muscles involves lying down and bringing the legs straight over the head until they touch the ground or floor behind the head. Done slowly, this exercise will work the abdominal muscles as well as loosen the lower back.

The importance of fitness in tennis cannot be overemphasized. All young players should find a coach or teacher who can show them other exercises that will get them ready to play the sport. It is hard to find a tennis coach who won't talk about fitness and keeping the muscles stretched and limber.

One other thing. Take a look at some of the top tennis players in the world. The wrist and forearm with which they swing the racket is almost always thicker and more muscular than their other arm. This is the result of years of practice and the hitting of thousands and thousands of tennis balls. If a young player hits enough tennis balls, he, too, will notice this development.

He can also do certain exercises to strengthen his wrist, forearm and shoulder when he is starting to play. a stronger arm will mean better control of the racket. If a young player wants to use weight training to strengthen the wrist and arm, he should definitely seek the advice of a coach or professional instructor who can give him the proper exercises with the equipment available.

Racket And Clothing

The first and foremost piece of equipment every tennis player needs is a racket. There are several things to consider when buying a racket. The first rule of thumb is to get the best quality racket that is right for you, and that you can afford.

Because there is no rule about the size and weight of a racket, the young player will have quite a variety from which to choose. By size, we are referring to the hitting surface—that is, the string portion that makes contact with the ball.

The smallest is the traditional size, the kind most tennis players have used for years. But now there is also a mid-size racket and an oversize racket with a very big hitting surface. Some feel the oversize racket helps young players pick up the game faster because the larger surface area cuts down on mis-hit balls. Everyone should try several different rackets before making a choice.

As important as the surface area are the weight and grip. For example, if a young player wants to use an oversize racket, he should ask for a *junior oversize*. That way, he will get a racket with the large surface area, but one of lighter weight and smaller grip.

A heavy racket is considered one that weighs 14 or 15 ounces, usually used by an adult player. The medium rackets weighs in the range of 13½ to 13¾ ounces, with the light racket going from 12½ to 13 ounces. The difference in weights might not seem much, but it can affect a player's game. A heavy racket can cause a player to tire. A racket that is too light can cause him to overhit the ball. Every new player must take his time when choosing a racket.

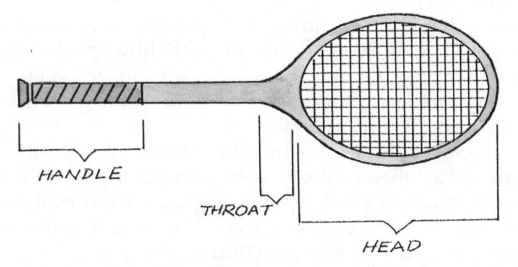

This is one style of tennis racket used today. It is made of wood and the strings are either nylon or gut. However, there are also aluminum rackets available, as well as those made of boron, graphite and Kevlar. Rackets also vary in weight and size. But the basic parts (handle, throat, face, head) are always the same.

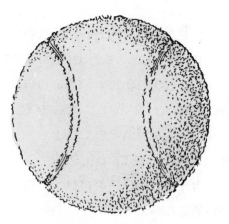

The tennis ball measures from 2½ to 2⅝ inches in diameter. It is a hollow rubber ball, covered with a felt-like fabric, which can be made of wool, nylon or Dacron. The more a ball is used, the less lively it becomes. Then it will not bounce as high or come off the racket as fast. So tennis balls should be changed often.

Years ago, all tennis rackets were made of wood. Today they are also made of aluminum, as well as some other materials, which cost more money. Wood or aluminum seem to be the best choices. They are strung with either nylon or gut. Nylon is probably better for young players because it doesn't require as much care as gut.

Tennis balls are made from rubber and covered with a fabric of wool, nylon or dacron. It's best to change balls often, because a worn ball won't bounce as high as a new one, and it will not react as well when hit.

Shoes should be well fitting and especially designed for tennis. In general, tennis shoes are low cut and lightweight, but there are different treads for different kinds of court surfaces. A knowledgeable person in a sporting goods store should know which shoe is made for which surface.

Clothing should be loose and comfortable. Men usually wear shorts and a pullover shirt. Women can wear short tennis skirts and sometimes shorts. Tennis clothing used to be mainly white, but today other light colors are used. Those playing outside will sometimes wear a hat to protect them from the sun. They can also wear a sweatband to keep the perspiration out of their eyes. Some players also like to wear sweatbands around their wrists.

The main things the new player must remember are to stay

physically fit; get a comfortable racket for his size, age and strength; and buy a pair of well-fitting tennis shoes. Then it is time to learn the game.

LEARNING TO PLAY THE GAME

Learning To Hit
The Forehand Stroke

The forehand stroke, or plain forehand, is perhaps the most basic stroke in tennis. A good, powerful forehand can be a formidable weapon in a tennis match. With the exception of the serve, the forehand is usually the hardest shot a player can make.

Before learning to hit the forehand, the beginning player must do something that will quickly become second nature; that is, grip the racket properly. This basic grip is the most important one, because any variations will come from it. To put it simply, a player learns the correct forehand grip by just shaking hands with the racket. It is also called the *Eastern grip*.

The new player should begin by grasping the racket at the throat with the nonhitting hand. Then, holding the racket straight out with the shorter strings pointing to the ground, he should

The basic Eastern tennis grip is achieved simply by shaking hands with the racket. The palm of the hand should be flat against the right side of the handle. This grip is used for the forehand drive and a number of other shots. Slight variations of the grip are used for the backhand and some types of serves.

22

place the palm of the hand against the flat side of the handle. He then closes the fingers and thumb around it, spreading the fingers comfortably apart. The thumb should rest at a point between the first and second fingers.

With the Eastern grip, the palm of the player's hand is always behind the racket as it moves forward in the forehand stroke. This gives the player a more powerful stroke and better control in placing the ball.

There are other types of grips that place the palm of the hand closer toward the top or bottom of the handle. But these grips will rob the player of power, especially on high and low forehand drives. Young players should start with the basic Eastern grip and learn to make adjustments from that.

Before going into the forehand stroke, all tennis players must know the basic stance. This is the position a player should be in while awaiting an opponent's shot. It is a little like an infielder in

A player waiting to receive a shot or serve must always be in the ready position. The ready stance means directly facing your opponent: feet shoulder-width apart, racket facing the net and held loosely, supported by the non-hitting hand. The knees should be bent slightly, your weight on the balls of your feet. When your opponent starts to swing, rock up onto your toes so you will be ready to move quickly in any direction, side to side or front to back.

baseball getting ready to field a ground ball. The player's body should be square to the net, feet spread comfortably apart. He should then grip the racket and point it toward the net. The non-hitting hand should hold the racket by the throat. This will take some of the weight off the hitting hand and arm.

The player should then crouch slightly, bend at the knees and keep his weight forward. When he sees his opponent ready to hit, he should rock onto the balls of his feet. That way, he will be ready to move quickly in any direction to get to the ball.

To hit the forehand stroke, or drive, the player begins by turning his body sideways to the net and shifting his weight to his rear foot. Watching the ball at all times, he brings his racket back, keeping his elbow slightly bent. The stroke is not unlike swinging at a baseball.

As the player starts his swing, he shifts his weight from his rear foot to his front foot. He brings his hips through the swing just in front of his arm. When he makes contact with the ball, it should be a bit out in front of him. Note how his eyes continue to watch the ball.

Next comes the hitting motion for the forehand drive. In some ways, it is similar to a baseball swing in that both the body and arms must work together for maximum power. When a right-handed player sees a ball coming to his forehand side, he goes into action. He begins the backswing by bringing the racket back on a flat plane, elbow close to the body, wrist straight and firm.

As he makes his backswing, he will also pivot on the ball of his right foot, turning his shoulders sideways to the net and shifting his weight back on that right foot. All the while, he must keep his eye only on the flight of the ball. When he is ready to swing, he will step into the ball, much like a batter in a baseball game.

The right-handed player will step with his left foot and point his toe in the direction of the right net post. The left-handed player will step with his right foot and point his toe toward the

A good, smooth follow-through is important to complete the stroke. The player's weight is now completely on the front foot and he is still watching the flight of the ball. From here, he can bring his rear foot forward and grab the throat of the racket with his non-hitting hand. He is then back in the ready position to return the next shot.

left net post. As the player begins the swing, he will pivot at the hip and shift his weight from his back to his front foot.

As he swings the racket, his elbow should be kept close to his body and bent slightly, his wrist held firm. The ball should be met in front of the body, somewhat in front of the left foot. For a flat drive, the racket should be straight up and down, connecting with the ball in the center of the face.

Once contact is made, the player must be sure to follow through, moving the racket along the arc of the swing and reaching forward. The heel of his back foot will often leave the court. The follow-through completes the stroke and helps give direction to the ball.

After he has completed a forehand drive, the player cannot relax. If he is at the center of the court, he must quickly return to the ready position. He should square his feet and grab the throat of the racket with his nonhitting hand. He is now ready to move after the next shot that comes his way.

The entire forehand drive should be made in a smooth, fluid motion. At the beginning, it is best not to worry about power. A young player should be more concerned with hitting the ball low over the net, keeping it in the court, and learning to place it on one side or the other. With practice, confidence and power will come.

Once a player has mastered the basic, flat forehand stroke, he can begin to do more things with it. The flatter he hits the ball, the more speed he will have in his drive. Speed describes how fast the ball travels through the air. Once it hits the ground and bounces, speed becomes *pace*. A flat drive will also have the most pace.

Many players like to put *topspin* on a forehand drive. Topspin will allow the ball to drop more sharply after it crosses the net and to bounce higher. To hit a forehand with topspin, the player

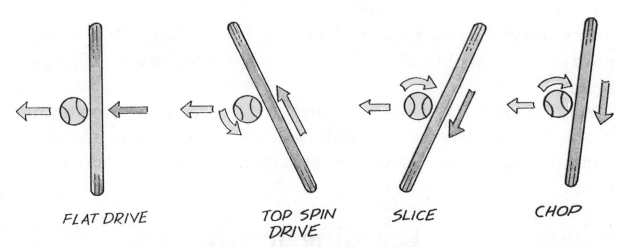

FLAT DRIVE   TOP SPIN   SLICE   CHOP
                  DRIVE

There are a number of ways to hit various shots. Each will cause the ball to move, spin, or slice in a certain manner. This illustration shows the angle and direction of the racket, as well as the spin of the ball on particular shots. These types of strokes are referred to often in the text.

should begin his stroke low and sweep upward. The racket contacts the ball and sweeps up across the top, giving it a forward spin. A topspin drive won't have the speed of a flat drive, but the ball is more likely to stay in the court and disrupt the rhythm of the opposing player.

Two other variations of the flat drive are the *slice* and the *chop*. The slice is achieved by hitting across the back of the ball at a downward angle. The chop comes from hitting down across the back of the ball in nearly the same motion used in chopping wood. A good slice will cause the ball to slide and curve when it bounces. The chop will have a short, heavy bounce with a lot of backspin and is often used to draw an opponent to the net.

But the good, powerful, flat forehand drive comes first. The perfect ball to hit this way is one that bounces waist high. If the ball is high or low, then the player must make a slight adjustment to his stroke. On a low ball, he should bend at the knees. Then, if he follows the same basic rules for the forehand drive, he will still be able to hit the ball with a level swing.

If the ball bounces high, from the waist to the shoulder, the player must raise the racket head on his backswing. While he will have to swing slightly downward on this stroke, he can still hit a tough, flat shot.

A good forehand drive is the first step to becoming a top tennis player. It takes practice, concentration and control of the racket. Once it's learned well, it will be a weapon you won't be afraid to use at any time during a match.

Learning To Hit
The Backhand Stroke

The backhand stroke, or backhand, is a very important part of playing a complete game of tennis. Some young players are afraid of the backhand and try to take every ball on the forehand side. But a good backhand can be just as strong a stroke as a forehand. In fact, there have been some professional players whose back-hands have been even better than their forehands.

The player here is about to make a running backhand drive using the one-hand backhand stroke. She has reached the ball, so the racket is already drawn back. Again the player tries to plant the rear foot before the stroke. Here she is stepping into the ball with her front foot and already beginning the weight shift.

To hit the backhand well, a player must make a slight adjustment from the basic Eastern grip used for the forehand. A right-handed player simply turns his hand about one-quarter turn to the left (counterclockwise) from the basic grip. The thumb is now behind the handle when the stroke is made, running diagonally on the flat side of the handle. A left-hander turns his hand a quarter turn to the right (clockwise) to achieve the same grip.

After a while, most players can change from the basic Eastern to the backhand grip by simply twirling the racket in their hands.

The one-hand follow-through is a little wider than the two-hand, which is a more compact stroke. Here, the player has stopped running and is about to return to the center of the court before getting ready for the next shot.

Because she has run for the ball, there is no time to really pivot at the hips. But she is still making a level swing and shifting all her weight onto her front foot.

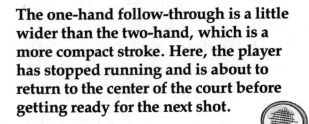

29

The newcomer may be better off by grasping it by the throat with the nonhitting hand and then making the grip adjustment.

The grip shift should be made as soon as a ball appears to be coming to the backhand side (which is, of course, across the body from the hitting hand). In many ways, the backhand stroke is much like the forehand. The backswing should be straight and parallel to the ground, with the hitting shoulder toward the net.

At the same time, the right-handed player will pivot on the ball of his left foot, then step forward with his right foot, pointing his toe at the right net post. The left-handed player will do just the opposite—pivot on the right foot and step forward with the left. With the backhand, the nonhitting hand may be used as a guide during the backswing.

The basic stroke should be made with the racket handle parallel to the ground. As the racket moves forward, the player will swing his weight forward, shifting it from the rear to the front foot. In a sense, he is leaning into the stroke. Contact with the ball should occur out in front of the body, perhaps 10 to 12 inches ahead of the front foot. The arm should be extended, with the elbow again kept close to the body during the stroke. Once again, the wrist should be straight and firm.

As with the forehand, the same rules apply for low and high balls. On low balls, the player will bend at the knees to get a level swing. In a sense, the player is bringing his waist down to the level of the ball. On high balls, the racket head should be raised to the level of the ball and the swing started from there. As with the high forehand drive, the swing will now be made on a slightly downward plane.

In recent years, many young players have taken to hitting a two-handed backhand stroke. This almost looks like a batter hitting a baseball. The two-handed backhand is often used by players who want to get more power into the stroke. Even some

30

The basic backhand drive can be hit with either one or two hands. This player is using the two-hand backhand. The motion of the swing is similar to swinging a bat at a baseball. The player has turned sideways, while bringing the racket back. As she brings it back, she grips the racket with her other hand. As with the forehand swing, the weight is shifted to the front foot.

The weight shift and pivot at the hips come a split second ahead of the arms. The stroke is made with both hands gripping the racket, eyes on the ball. Again, the ball is hit when it is still slightly in front of the player.

Both hands are kept on the racket during the follow-through. The head is still down, eyes on the ball, and all the weight is now on the front foot. After the stroke, the player will bring her back leg forward to assume the ready position.

31

men and women professionals use the two-handed shot. This is something a young player will have to decide for himself. There is no real drawback to the two-handed stroke, with the exception that it limits a player's reach to a small degree. But it is also a stroke that can be hit with power and accuracy.

With the two-handed backhand, the right-handed player will use his right hand as the bottom hand on the racket. Conversely, the left-handed player's left hand will be the bottom hand. The bottom hand should use the Eastern backhand grip, while the top hand uses the basic Eastern forehand grip.

The rest of the stroke is similar to the conventional backhand. As the ball approaches, the player pivots and turns as he begins his backswing. Only this time he places his free hand on the handle of the racket, just above the primary hitting hand, which has shifted to the backhand grip. He then swings in the same manner, shifting his weight from his rear foot to his front one. The only difference is that he keeps both hands on the racket and uses both arms to complete the stroke.

As with the one-handed backhand, the elbows should be kept close to the body and the player must follow-through, again keeping both hands on the racket. At the top of the follow-through, the player may let go of the racket with his top hand and resume the ready stance position for the next shot.

It takes a great deal of practice to master both the forehand and backhand strokes. Playing against someone is certainly a fine way to learn, but sometimes it's better to just go out and hit stroke after stroke. Find a practice board or wall that can be used as a silent partner. The wall will return ball after ball, allowing the player to practice his strokes repeatedly.

By combining hours with a practice board and hours on the court, you will begin to master both the forehand and backhand strokes. The next step is learning how to serve.

Learning How To Serve

Because every single point of a tennis match begins with a serve, it's no secret that a player with a powerful service game will have a tremendous advantage. He can win many points right off his serve. A good serve that goes right past an opponent without being returned is called an *ace*. A serve that is returned into the net or out of bounds is a *service winner*.

Conversely, a serve that either goes into the net or lands outside the service court is called a *fault*. The server then has a second chance. Two faults, called a *double fault*, result in a loss of a point. A serve that hits the top of the net and then falls into the service court is called a *let*. The server can then take that serve over again.

During a match, each player takes turns serving one whole game. He will always serve first from the right side behind the baseline into the left service court on his opponent's side. The next serve will be from the left side of the baseline into right-hand service court.

There are two basic grips used in the serve. The first is the Eastern grip, the same one used to hit the forehand drive. It can be used to hit a flat, hard serve. Later, when the young player becomes more confident and wants to try to put spin and slice on his service, he can use the *Continental grip*. The Continental grip is halfway between the Eastern forehand and Eastern backhand grips. The right-handed player will simply turn his hand about an eighth of a turn to the left (counterclockwise) from the forehand grip. The left-handed player will turn his hand clockwise. This will place the palm of the hand on top of the handle.

Next comes the stance. The server should stand just behind the baseline and very close to the center mark on the court. As a rule, a right-handed player serving from the right side of the center mark into the opposite left service court (also called the *deuce court*) will stand very close to the center mark. When serving from the left side into the right service court (also called the *ad court*), he will stand perhaps two or three steps from the center mark.

The right-handed server begins by standing almost sideways to the net facing the right sideline. His left, or front, foot should be just an inch or two behind the baseline, with his toes pointing to the right net post. His right, or rear, foot is usually about 18 inches behind the left and more parallel to the line. The important thing is that the server feels comfortable and balanced as he prepares for the toss.

While tossing the ball in the air may seem simple enough, it must be done just right, for it is one of the keys to successful service. If the ball and racket do not meet at just the right spot, a good serve is nearly impossible. So a poor toss will spoil the serve before it really begins.

A perfect serve can result only if the ball is hit in the split second that it is not moving. That is the exact moment it stops rising to begin its fall. If the toss is too high, then the ball will already be falling rapidly when it is hit. A low toss will force the player to shorten his swing, and he will lose power.

For the right-handed player, the toss should begin with the ball held lightly in the fingertips of the left hand. The forearm should be parallel to the ground, the elbow in close to the body. The toss is made in a smooth upward motion (don't move the hand down and then back up again), with the ball released at about eye level. It should go straight up.

The toss should not go directly over the server's head. To make a powerful serve possible, the ball must be hit when it is just in front of the server's head as he faces the net. At point of impact, the racket will have just passed a vertical position. One way to check the toss is to let the ball come down without hitting it. A

This is the position from which the player begins the basic serve. The back is straight, the front foot just behind the service line. The toss will begin from waist height.

The toss is all-important and takes practice. For a righthand serve, a good toss will be just to the right of the head and a few inches in front of the body. It should only go as high as the top of the racket, since it should be hit the moment it reaches its maximum height and before it begins to fall.

As the ball is released, the server bends both knees forward, loops his racket back, and shifts his weight to the rear foot. The serving motion itself has been described as being similar to throwing a baseball from the out-field.

Here the server is about to bend his wrist back to get extra snap into the stroke. He has shifted his weight to the front and is up on his toes for more power.

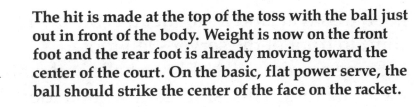

The hit is made at the top of the toss with the ball just out in front of the body. Weight is now on the front foot and the rear foot is already moving toward the center of the court. On the basic, flat power serve, the ball should strike the center of the face on the racket.

A smooth follow-through is also important to the serve. The player's eyes are rooted on the ball and he is set to come to the center of the court or to charge the net. Once he has made the hit, he can immediately step over the baseline onto the court.

good toss will land in about an eight-inch radius just inside the court in front of the server's left foot.

Some servers will hold two balls in their hand when they make their first toss. This isn't really a good idea. The second ball should be placed in the pocket of the shorts. The rules do not say that every toss must be hit. A server can allow a bad toss to simply drop and then toss it again. It does not count as a fault. During the toss, the server must also make sure his front foot does not touch the baseline. If it does, a *foot fault* will be called, and the serve is no good, no matter where it lands.

Now it's time for the actual service stroke. There are several things a good server must be able to do. First, he must hit an accurate serve with power. Then he must place the serve in a particular spot in the server's court that might just catch the returner off balance. Third, he must put slice and spin on the serve.

Because a server gets two tries, he can put everything he has on his first serve. That is when he attempts an ace or a service winner. If he needs his second serve, he must be sure to put the ball into play so he doesn't lose the point on a double fault.

The basic flat, hard serve is made with the Eastern grip. The actual serving stroke has often been compared to an outfielder in baseball making a long throw to home plate. The same kind of overhand motion is used. When he is ready to begin, the server stands with his weight balanced on both feet. His racket is in front of him, pointed toward the net with the face at about head level and the butt pointing toward the waist. The ball is in the fingertips waiting to be tossed. It should be touching the strings or throat of the racket.

The backswing begins at the same time the toss is made. At this point, the server also shifts his weight to his back foot. The arm action on the backswing is the same as if an outfielder were getting ready to make that long throw. The server breaks his wrist

Another angle shows the position of the feet as the toss is made. Note how the weight is already beginning to shift from rear to front.

As the server begins the stroke he has bent his wrist and has come onto his toes. His weight is now moving forward, so he can lean into the shot.

Just after the overhand hit is made, the server begins stepping onto the court with his rear foot. If any part of his foot touches the baseline before the hit is made, a foot fault is called and the serve is no good, no matter where it lands.

and bends his arm at the elbow until the racket is almost vertical to the ground.

At this point, he will bring the racket upward and forward with a whipping motion. At the same time, he should shift his weight from the rear to the front foot. While he is doing this, he must keep his eye on the ball and nothing else. The contact should be made right in the center of the strings. The arm and racket should be fully extended at point of contact.

As with all strokes, the follow-through is very important. The racket must continue its downward course, following the ball toward the receiving court. At the same time, the heel of the front foot will rise from the forward motion, and the back foot will slide forward, swinging past the front foot. This completes the weight shift. By this time, the racket should be down past the opposite side of the body.

With the flat serve, the ball will not spin or twist. But it can be a serve of tremendous power. If it is placed correctly in a spot where the returner is not expecting it, there is a good chance it will pass him for an ace, or at least become a service winner.

Once a player has confidence in his flat serve, he is ready to try some other type of service. One common variety is the *slice serve*. For the slice, the Continental grip is used. The stance is the same as the flat serve, but the toss is different. With the slice serve, the right-handed player must toss the ball a bit more to the right.

Then, instead of hitting the ball dead center, he will hit it on the upper right of center. The server will hit the ball more from the outside down, turning his wrist slightly to the right as he makes contact. This allows the racket strings to cut across the surface of the ball, giving it spin and slice.

A right-handed player's slice will spin left to right and will curve to the left as it travels through the air. When it hits, it will bounce sharply to the right. A left-hander's slice will act in just the opposite way. The slice is often used as a second serve after a fault. Because the second serve is not normally as hard as the first, a slice will make it just a little more difficult to return.

Another popular serve is called the *American Twist*. It is also known as a topspin or kick serve. The American Twist is generally hit using the backhand grip. Again, the toss is important. This time the ball should be tossed to the left and slightly back. At point of impact, it should be above the left ear of a right-handed server. This time, the ball should be hit on the upper left side.

The server must arch his back to get the racket in position to get the proper spin on the ball. This time, when he follows through, his racket should come down on the rightside of his body. When an American Twist serve hits the surface of the court, it will bounce or kick high and to the right side. It's considered a good serve against a right-handed opponent with a weak backhand.

The slice and twist serves both call for a great deal of wrist action and should not be overdone by young players. All young players should master the basic flat serve before trying either variation. Young players should also remember that the American Twist can put a lot of strain on both the back and elbow. The arm action is almost like a pitcher throwing a screwball. Young players trying the twist serve all the time could wind up with back or elbow injuries.

Service Strategy

The service courts are 13½ feet wide and 21 feet deep. That's a pretty big target for the server to put the ball in play, and putting the ball in play is the first thing the young or beginning player should try to achieve. Don't worry about serving to the corners, or putting a twist serve in deep. Try to get the ball in play with increasing speed and pace.

It should be obvious that the more first serves you can put into play, the better chance you have to win the point. Accuracy on the first serve is very important. Since the second serve is softer, it will give your opponent a much better chance to hit a winner. Of course, a missed second serve means a double fault and a point just given away. Most tennis players hate to double fault.

The more a player practices his serve, the more he should concentrate on hitting the ball deep, toward the rear of the service court. A short serve gives the opponent a better chance for a strong return. Once a player can hit a strong serve, keep it in the court and get it deep, then he can start to place the ball.

In general, the server tries to keep his opponent off balance and guessing where the next serve will be. He should hit the majority of the serves to his opponent's weaker side. If his opponent has a weak backhand, nearly 80 percent of his serves should be placed toward the backhand side. The other 20 percent to the forehand will be enough to make the opponent guess.

Occasionally, the server can mix things up by hitting a low, short serve that will bring his opponent in toward the net. Even if the return is made, the server may have a chance to hit a winner deep to the opposite side. Most players follow a pattern of blasting their first serve, looking for that ace or winner. If they fault, they go to the slice or spin on their second, looking for a tricky placement of the softer serve.

Unlike practicing the forehand and backhand, it's not a good idea to practice the serve too often against a board or wall. While serving against a wall might give a feel for the toss and technique, it won't help when it comes to getting that first blast into the court. Instead, a player wanting to practice service should simply get a bucket of balls, find an empty court, and begin serving, over and over again. Practice may not make perfect, but it will certainly make a sound, improving player.

Service Return

With all these cannonball serves rocketing across the net, what about the poor guy on the other side? Better not forget about him, for every tennis player must be able to return a strong serve as well as produce one. There are some basic rules for returning serves that all young players should know.

For openers, no one should take the service return lightly. If a player has a poor return of service, he will probably be beaten by a strong server every time out. That's how important it is to be able to handle every kind of serve.

When waiting for the serve, the player should assume the ready position. His feet should be spread apart, racket held in front, the nonhitting hand on the throat for added support. As the server tosses the ball and begins his backswing, the returner should rock onto the balls of his feet. That way he is ready to move quickly in either direction as soon as the ball flashes across the net. There is no substitute for quickness when returning serves.

Most young players will stand just inside the baseline while waiting to take a first serve. Some pros, when facing a very hard server, will stand behind the baseline. But a young player should position himself in front of it. Until he knows the type of server he is facing, he should stand midway between the center mark and the sideline. Once he sees what is coming at him, he may decide to play more to one side or the other.

While waiting to make the return, always concentrate on the server. Watch the ball closely. Sometimes the toss will give away whether a flat serve, slice or twist is coming. That will make it a little easier to anticipate the pace and direction of the ball.

Hold the racket with the basic Eastern grip while awaiting the serve, but be ready to go the Eastern backhand grip in a split second. If the server is a very hard hitter, the return may have to be made with more of a blocking type stroke. Instead of taking a full swing, the returner should just hold the racket so the face is vertical, or straight up and down. He should be sure to keep his wrist firm as contact is made. Despite the short stroke, the force of the serve will cause the return to be made with more than enough power.

The primary concern of the returner is to keep the ball in play. If he hits it into the net or out of bounds, the server has won the point. A second concern is to return the ball deep. That will prevent the server from rushing the net and perhaps getting an easy winner on his next shot. A deep return will keep the server closer to the baseline and allow the returner to get into position for the next shot.

After making a deep return, the player should quickly move to center court near the baseline and be ready for whatever might come next. Once the returner has confidence that he can handle his opponent's serves, he can begin to do even more with the ball.

For example, if he sees the server rushing the net behind his serve, he can try to lob the ball over his head. Or when he moves in closer to take the softer second serve, he might try for a winner of his own. He may even want to put a slice or topspin on his return.

A good return game goes hand in hand with a strong service game. It's very difficult to win without being good at both of these important skills.

Learning Some Additional Strokes

Learning the basic forehand and backhand strokes, as well as the serve, will go a long way toward making a beginner a real tennis player. However, there are a few other points about the

The running forehand uses most of the same rules as the basic forehand. As the player runs toward the ball, he should have begun his backswing, so the racket is ready. The backswing is a bit shorter than the basic forehand swing. The player should also learn to time his run so he can plant his rear foot just before he makes the stroke.

basic strokes that must be learned, and there are some special shots that every new player should know.

The form for the basic forehand and backhand is simple enough. There is the backswing, the shift of weight, the swing and the follow-through. But these things aren't quite the same if the player has to run hard to reach the ball before making his shot. Therefore, every newcomer to the sport must learn how to make the forehand and backhand shot on the run, as well as standing still.

From the ready position, a player moving to the right should pivot on the ball of his right foot and take the first step with his

With his rear foot planted, the player begins the stroke, again watching the ball. He will shift his weight the same way he does with the basic forehand. If the player has a long way to run and must lunge for the ball, then he must make the stroke almost completely with his arm. He will not have time for the weight shift.

The player should make a smooth follow-through. But instead of going right back to the ready position, he should take several quick steps toward the center of the court before getting ready. Otherwise, he can be caught out of position on the return.

left. Moving to the left is just the opposite, pivot on the left foot and step with the right. As a rule, a player should take short, quick steps, moving on the balls of his feet.

In going after a ball, always begin your backswing as you start to run. Don't wait until you reach the ball to start your backswing. With the racket ready, it's just a matter of adjusting steps so you can step into the shot with your front foot. Then, once again, shift your weight and follow through as you make the stroke. To be on the wrong foot or between steps when it's time to swing will result in a weak shot or an error.

The same rules apply to the running backhand. Move quickly on the balls of your feet, time your steps and get the racket back before you reach the ball.

The Volley

A volley is the name given to a stroke made before the ball hits the ground. It may be a forehand or backhand stroke, but any time racket meets ball before the ball hits the ground, it's a volley. There was a time when most top tennis stars played strong serve and volley games. That meant that the server usually rushed the net behind his serve, hoping to hit a winner off a volley.

That type of game made for many short rallies, with the point decided with just one or two strokes after the serve. Today, many matches consist of longer rallies, with players hitting ground strokes from the baseline. However, there still are times when a player charges the net, looking for a winning volley.

The volley is usually hit anywhere from between the back line of the service courts to the net. The ideal volley is made on a high ball close to the net, which can be hit down and with power. It is usually a winner.

Further back, the volley is not taken as a full stroke. There is little backswing and a less-than-normal follow-through. Like the

When hitting a low volley, it is important that the player get the entire body down and not just lower the racket head. Here, the player is bending at the knees, even though she has had to run for the ball.

service return, it is more of a blocking stroke. The power comes from the speed of the shot to be returned. Because the volley must be hit quickly, a player doesn't always have the time to turn his body and get into the classic position for a forehand or backhand.

Instead, he must just turn his shoulders and bring the racket back into position. The important thing is to take a crisp, short stroke and keep the wrist very firm. A strong, firm wrist will help to get maximum power into the stroke. The backhand volley is usually hit a bit further out in front of the body than the forehand because it takes more time to bring the racket around to the backhand side. As with the regular backhand and forehand strokes, the player bends at the knees to hit a low volley.

The volley is always an attacking move. A player approaching the net to hit a volley is looking for a winner. He should always try to hit the shot deep and at an angle toward the corner of the

Here is a player hitting a backhand low volley the correct way. He has bent down low at the knees and has the head of the racket level. Notice how intently he is watching the ball.

court. That way, it will be more difficult to return. Also, the attacking player will have more of a chance to get back into position for a return.

By carefully watching your opponent, you will learn to figure out what kind of shot is coming at you. That way, you'll have a better idea when to attack at the net and perhaps hit a winning volley.

A *half volley* is the name given a ball hit a split second after it strikes the court. It's almost like an infielder picking up a short hop. Unlike the volley, the half volley is not an attacking stroke. It's a stroke a player needs during a match when he suddenly has a ball coming right at his feet.

The drop shot is hit with a soft touch. The player hits under the ball, giving it back-spin. So it's a good idea to bend at the knees to make it easier to come up under the ball.

On the half volley, contact should be made well out in front of the body. Whether it's taken on the forehand or backhand side, always bend low at the knees. In fact, on some half volleys the knee of your back leg must be just 12 or so inches off the court. The stroke should be short and compact, with contact made after the ball has bounced just a few inches. The speed of the ball coming off the court should enable the shot to be crisp and firm.

The Drop Shot

The drop shot is used to catch an opponent off guard. It's a soft shot with backspin that drops just over the net and dies there. It's generally used when the opponent is deep in the court and will have a long run to reach it. The ball is almost always hit from the forecourt.

By slicing the racket under the ball, the player will make the ball go over the net with backspin and have very little forward bounce. In fact, it may even bounce back toward the net, making it even more difficult for an opponent to reach the ball for a return.

The shot itself is hit with the face of the racket tilted up. Whether the ball is hit from the forehand or backhand side, the swing should be a short, slicing chop across the underside, causing backward spin. This takes away any forward bounce and may even cause the ball to bounce back toward the net.

In almost all instances, the shot must be taken close to the net and with the opponent deep in his own court. If it is taken from too deep or if the opponent is too close to the net, the drop shot can backfire and lead to a winning return.

The Lob

The lob is a delicate placement shot that takes a soft touch and good judgment. It is used when an opponent has rushed the net and is looking for a winning volley. A good lob will arch high over his head and land just inside the baseline. The opponent will have to run hard to reach the shot. Even if he does, he usually will not be in a position for a strong return.

Since the lob is a ground stroke, it must be hit off a bounce. The stance and grip are the same for a regular stroke. But, again, the backswing and follow-through are short and compact. Like the drop shot, the lob is hit with the face of the racket tilted back. Unlike the drop, there is no spin or slice on the ball. The wrist should be firm and the follow-through upward to direct the path of the ball.

The lob is often a defensive maneuver used when a player is out of position and open to a winner from his opponent. Instead of a weak ground stroke that the opponent at the net can volley home, the lob is used to get a player out of trouble and allow him the time to get a good position on the court.

The Overhead Smash

The overhead smash is the answer to a poor lob. In a sense, it's almost like a serve, but it can come from any point on the court. The grip and direction of the stroke are nearly identical to the serve. There is also a similar shift of weight from the rear to the front foot. Only the backswing and follow-through are slightly different, they are both a little more compact.

To hit a proper overhead, the player must get to the ball quickly. He must be there, waiting for it to come down. The overhead is not a stroke that can be hit on the run. The ball should be hit out in front of your body, even more so than the serve. Timing is all important, too. Otherwise, an overhead smash can easily be hit out of bounds or even up into, the stands.

As a rule, the overhead should be hit on a fly, before it bounces. This way, the other player won't have much time to react. Only

An overhead smash is much like a serve. It takes good timing, since the ball should be hit on the fly. The trick is to get in position under the ball as quickly as possible. Have the racket already drawn back so you're ready to make the stroke as soon as you get under the ball.

The motion is much like a serve in that the wrist breaks backwards to generate snap and power in the stroke. And never take your eyes off the ball, not even for a split second.

Try to make the hit just in front of your body. The weight shift should be from rear to front. The arm should be fully extended with the shoulder also leaning into the smash. And don't forget to follow-through.

hit an overhead on a bounce when there is not enough time to hit it on the fly. But, hit well either way, an overhead smash is a great offensive weapon. If placed right, it is a shot that is almost always a sure winner.

Learning Singles Strategy

Singles tennis is a total one-on-one situation. Each player is trying to master his opponent. He must hit sure, firm ground strokes and keep the ball in play. He should go for winners when he sees an opening and try to keep his errors to a minimum.

For beginners, the best strategy is to keep the ball in play. More matches are lost on errors (hitting the ball into the net or out of bounds) than are won by hitting winners. This is even true of the pros. So at the beginning, each player should work on hitting down the middle and keeping the ball deep.

Then, as his basic skills improve, the new player can become more daring. But even as he begins to aim more shots at the corners and move his opponent around, he must still try to force the other guy to make the error.

Concentration is always very important in a tennis match. The best players always talk about "mental toughness." A tennis player must work for each point and concentrate on making every shot. He cannot let anyone break his concentration, not his opponent or the people watching the match. If he is losing, he must still work hard to get back in the match. He has to think this way right up to the final point.

As a beginning player, you must also learn to watch your opponent closely. Always look for weaknesses you might be able to exploit. For example, if your opponent runs around every ball and tries to hit it with his forehand, you should try even harder to play to his backhand. If your opponent doesn't seem to want to rush the net, then you should try drop shots whenever you have the chance. If your opponent is trying short lobs, the overhead smash should work well. If your opponent is drilling balls hit right at you, then move him around the court.

There are all kinds of little things to look for. The good player can spot a weakness in an opponent quickly. Another sound piece of advice is not to tamper with a winning game. If a style of play is working well, don't change it. For example, if hitting deep ground strokes from the baseline is winning the match, don't suddenly decide to rush the net and look for the volley.

If that same baseline game isn't working at all, then it's time to try something different. Perhaps rushing the net will turn the game around, or perhaps hitting short drop shots will make a difference. Whenever a particular strategy isn't working, then by all means try to change the rhythm of the game. Make the guy on the other side of the net change his tactics.

Another thing to watch for is the court surface. Before a match even starts, always know the court. A clay court is much slower than a cement court. The ball will bounce differently, and the pace of the ground strokes won't be the same. Try to determine this during warm-ups because the court surface may cause you to change your game. Traditionally, the fast court lends itself to serve and volley tennis, with quick points and many winners. The slow court often leads to baseline games with long rallies. Patience and keeping the ball in play often win a slow court game.

Of course, there is no substitute for experience and for practice. As with most sports, learning to play tennis well takes time. It's a game that can be played by boys and girls, youngsters, adults and senior citizens. Everyone who plays should be competitive and try to win, but they should also enjoy the game. Above all, the game of tennis should always be fun.

Learning Doubles Strategy

Most of the lessons so far have involved singles play. But doubles tennis is a very popular version of the game. Playing doubles involves teamwork and a whole different set of strategies.

Whereas singles put a great deal of emphasis on ground strokes and baseline rallies, doubles is very different. Much of the play takes place at and around the net. In fact, much of the time all four players come to the net for lightning-quick exchanges.

In a sense, doubles can be a faster game than singles, especially as far as quickness and reflex actions are concerned. All the

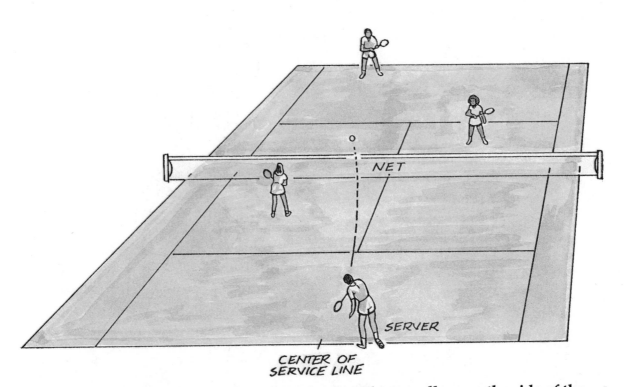

NET

SERVER

CENTER OF
SERVICE LINE

Doubles is a different kind of game than singles. The two alleys on the side of the court are in play for doubles. This is the basic position of the players during the serve.

speed, of course, requires great teamwork between the doubles partners. If a player doesn't know where his partner is at all times, the team will be in trouble.

The doubles court is nine feet wider than the singles court, with a 4½ foot alley on each side. As a general rule, each partner covers one half of the court, which adds up to a smaller area of coverage than in singles play. Just because a player is good in singles doesn't mean he will be a good doubles player. Some just never pick up the teamwork.

Good doubles teams are generally those that have played together for a long time. There is no substitute for experience, and the better the two players know each other's games, the better doubles team they will make. Most good doubles teams are very vocal, constantly shouting, ''Yours,'' or ''Mine,'' on tough shots down the middle or on lobs.

Though each player in doubles usually covers one-half of the court, strategies sometimes change. Here the player closest to the net is cutting into his partner's side of the court to make a shot. The partner, seeing this, is crossing over to cover the part of the court that has been vacated. That's teamwork, a very important part of the doubles' game.

There are times when both players can reach a ball. It should be taken by the player with the best shot in that situation. Both players must know this immediately, especially if there is no time to shout it out. For example, if a ball is hit down the middle and the player on the left has a perfect angle for a strong forehand, he should take it. His partner might have been able to reach it with a backhand, but the stroke wouldn't have been as strong.

Sometimes, the two partners must cross over. Suppose the

player on the left side of the court is close to the net. Suddenly there is a lob hit over his head. Instead of that player racing back for the ball, his partner on the right side can run behind him for the overhead. As he does this, the player from the left side must cross over the to the right side of the court to cover the area his partner has left.

Doubles partners must try to keep the entire court covered at all times. There are times when a player will make a sudden lunge into his partner's territory, but he will only do this if he feels he can hit a sure winner. One example could have the player on the right side playing midway back on the court. The ball comes over the net and looks as if it will bounce at his feet. Suddenly his partner on the left side lunges across court and hits a forehand volley for a winner.

Even though his partner could have probably returned the shot, the other player saw a chance for a winner and took the gamble. Again, these are things that come with experience.

Doubles partners must alternate as servers. The partner with the best service game cannot serve all the time. Also, if a player's serve touches his partner on the way over the net, it is a fault. The receiving team can also alternate. If one player is much better at returning serves, he can take every service, just switching sides with his partner.

In most doubles matches, the server comes to the net as quickly as he can. One partner generally plays a step or two closer to the net than the other. Who plays the closest is sometimes determined by height and reflexes. A tall, quick player can be a tough opponent at the net.

Since most doubles points end quickly, the serve and service return are very important. The server should concentrate on getting his first serve into play. A soft, second serve will give too much of an advantage to the receiving team. The receiving team should try to keep their returns as low as possible. One good maneuver is to hit the return at the feet of the server, who will be coming to the net. A well-hit return at the server's feet will usually result in a weak shot and put his team on the defensive.

Doubles teams look for sharp volleys from close in, always trying to hit down on the ball with power for possible winners. There is rarely a long rally in a good doubles match. For that reason, the players must concentrate very hard on their shots, their position and their partners.

Whether a newcomer to tennis chooses to play singles or doubles is up to him. Most players do both. The fun is just learning and playing the game. Tennis is not a difficult sport to learn. A young player just starting out can be hitting the ball over the net very quickly. But like other sports, it takes a great deal of practice to become a good player. An experienced coach can be a big help, as well as playing against others who are just as good or maybe even a little better.

The important thing is to learn the basic strokes correctly and use them as building blocks to a better, faster game. Hitting that service ace or a baseline winner, making a fine shot on a return or throwing up a perfect lob are all things that will make you feel great! Because then you'll know you learned the sport well.

Tennis is a fast, healthy sport that can make you feel good and keep you in top physical condition. If you practice hard and become good enough, you may want to enter tournaments. Who knows, the day may come when you're a winner, collecting your prize at center court.

Glossary

Ace   A serve that wins a point by landing in the service court without being returned by the opponent.

Advantage   A scoring term used when a player has a one-point lead in a game that has been tied at 40–40.

American Twist   A type of serve that requires the server to put topspin on the ball, giving it a high kick when it strikes the court.

Backhand   A stroke used by a player to hit a ball on the opposite side, away from his natural hitting hand. The racket is brought across the body and can be held with one or two hands.

Backswing   The first part of a stroke in which the player brings the racket back into the hitting position.

Baseline   The back line at each end of the tennis court.

Continental grip   A grip that is halfway between the basic forehand and backhand grips. It's often used for serving.

Court   The lined surface with a net in the middle upon which tennis is played.

Crossover   A doubles maneuver in which one partner crosses to the other side of the court to get the ball while his or her partner crosses the other way to protect the vacated portion.

Deuce   A scoring term used to describe a tie game at 40–40 or at any point thereafter.

Double fault   Term used to describe the loss of a point after two straight serving attempts have failed to put the ball in play.

Doubles   The form of tennis played on a wider court than singles and with two people on a side.

Drop shot   A short groundstroke carefully placed to drop just beyond the net with little or no bounce.

Eastern grip   The basic forehand grip, achieved by simply shaking hands with the racket. Moving the hand a quarter turn to the right converts it to the Eastern backhand grip.

Error   A mis-hit ball that causes a player to lose a point.

Fault   Term used when a serve fails to land in the proper court to put the ball in play.

Foot fault   Another service term used to describe a disallowed serve due to the server's foot making contact with the baseline.

Forehand   A stroke used by a player to hit balls on the same side as his hitting hand. With the forehand, the racket is usually held with just one hand.

Groundstrokes   Term used to describe any stroke used to hit a ball after it has bounced.

Half volley A stroke in which the ball is hit a split-second after it has bounced, or on a short hop.

Let A serve that goes into play but has touched the net on the way over. The server is allowed to take it over again.

Lob A ball intentionally hit high over an opponent's head and designed to land just inside the baseline.

Love A scoring term that refers to zero, whether it be points, games, or sets.

Mental toughness A kind of concentration that allows a player to be at his best stroke after stroke, game after game, set after set.

Mixed doubles A doubles match in which the partners consist of a man and a woman on each side.

Overhead smash The answer to a bad lob. A hard forehand stroke of a high ball, hit almost identically to the serve.

Passing shot A volley or groundstroke that goes past an opponent for a winner without being hit.

Rally Term given to a long point in which each player hits the ball many times before the point is decided.

Ready stance The position a player uses while waiting for his opponent's shot. His feet are spread comfortably apart, knees bent slightly, racket in front, with the non-hitting hand holding it by the throat.

Serve The way the ball is put into play on every point. Players take turns serving in every other game.

Serve and volley Name given to a style of play in which the server charges the net and tries to end the point quickly.

Service court The area in which a serve must land to put the ball in play. There are two service courts on each side of the net.

Set Part of a match that ends when one player wins at least six games. But he must have a two-game lead at that point to win.

Singles A tennis match played with just one player on each side of the net.

Slice A term used to describe a ball hit with enough spin to make it curve in the air and kick right or left when it lands.

Tiebreaker Fairly new method to break a tie when a set is even at six games apiece. There are several types of tiebreakers, the most common being five and seven-point. The first player to reach that number of points wins the game and the set.

Topspin Term used to describe a ball hit with forward rotation, causing it to arc downward and then bounce high.

Toss The act of throwing the ball in the air just before hitting the serve.

Volley Any shot in which the ball is hit in the air before it bounces on the court.

Winner A serve or shot that results in a point being won.